ICT

Graham Parton

Acknowledgements

The author and publisher would like to thank the staff and children of Kent College Infant and Junior School and Chartham County Primary School for their much appreciated contributions of work and artwork during the writing of this book.

The author would also like to thank his wife and family for their support during the writing and preparation of this book.

Recording sounds (page 49).

© 2000 Belair Publications, on behalf of the author.

Apex Business Centre, Boscombe Road, Dunstable, LU5 4RL.
Email: belair@belair-publications.co.uk

Editor: Elizabeth Miles
Photography: Roger Brown and Kelvin Freeman

Design: Jane Conway
Cover design: Ed Gallagher

- *DinoDon* used by permission of aol.com.
- *Dazzle* used by permission of Silica Software Systems and Granada Learning Ltd.
- *Cambridge Talking Books* used by permission of Sherston Software.
- *Textease* used by permission of Softease Limited.
- Screen shots from *My World for Windows*, by Semerc Software, courtesy of Granada Learning Ltd.
- Screen shots from *Yahoo!* courtesy of Yahoo! Inc.
- Screen shots from *Counting Pictures* courtesy of BlackCat, a division of Granada Learning Ltd.
- *Superlogo* courtesy of Longman Logotron Ltd.

First published in 2000 by Belair Publications.
Reprinted 2001.
Reprinted 2003.

Every effort has been made to contact copyright holders of material used in this publication. If any copyright holder has been overlooked, we should be pleased to make any necessary arrangements.

British Library Cataloguing in Publication Data. A catalogue record for this publication is available from the British Library.

ISBN 0 94788 251-0

Contents

Language and Literacy

Mathematics

Science and Humanities

Music and Art

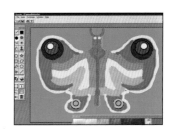

Introduction

The aim of this series is to provide resource material covering all the main areas of young children's learning. Each book is a 64-page full colour resource, designed specifically for educators, which provides practical 'hands on' activities suitable for working with the under-fives. They also provide a variety of starting points to encourage and promote creative play.

Written by professionals working in early years education, each book is organised into popular early years themes providing ideas to develop the linguistic, mathematical, scientific, creative, environmental, and personal and social areas of learning. The key learning intentions are provided for each theme.

Full colour photography offers ideas and inspiration for presenting and developing children's individual work with creative ideas for display. An additional feature of each book is the 'Home Links' section. This provides extension ideas and activities for children to develop at home for each theme.

Information and Communication Technology is a part of our everyday lives – we use ICT at home and at work and children are becoming increasingly adept at using computers and technology. Children regularly program video recorders, tune-in a television set, go online to order a book, and play computer and console games.

As an increasingly important part of our lives, it is important to teach ICT skills in exciting and stimulating ways. This book aims to show how young children can be given easy access to computers and how they can soon gain confidence in using a range of hardware and software. It also offers a valuable range of stimulating and exciting activities. The programs used can be found in most classrooms – for example, any word processor can be used with a concept keyboard and any spreadsheet program can be used for making graphs. A list of suggested software can be found on page 64.

By using the activities in this book, those who are less confident in teaching ICT to young children will be surprised to discover how ICT can be taught effectively by anyone – teachers, teaching assistants, and parents or carers alike. ICT can be a very creative medium for children to learn from and, with a little imagination, teachers can plan and implement motivating ICT activities for young children.

Creating a Computer Area

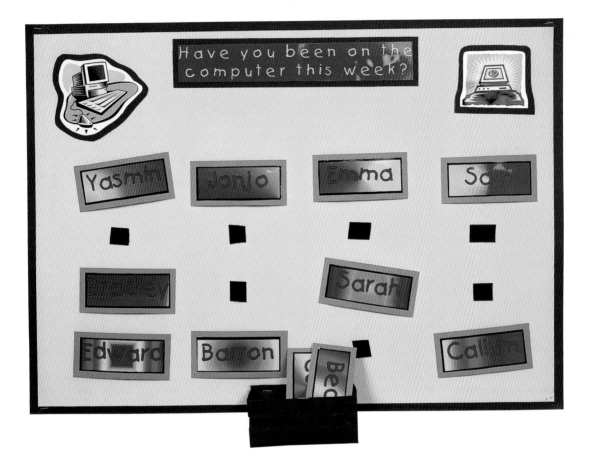

- Make the computer area as interesting as possible by adding bright backing paper and colourful images to display boards (see photograph on pages 6–7).

- Give the area a fun and stimulating theme and title, such as 'Computer Games' or 'Dinosaurs on the internet' and display the children's work associated with these themes. Try to change the theme regularly to encourage the children to visit the area.

- Create a covered board with fabric-fastenings and entitle it 'Have you been on the computer today?'. Make some cards with the children's names on and attach a fabric fastening to the back of each. These can be used to check who has been on the computer and, more importantly, who has not!

- Encourage the children to cut out pictures of computer hardware, such as monitors, keyboards, mice and speakers from catalogues and magazines. Label and display the pictures in the computer area.

- Find pictures of other items linked to ICT, such as tape recorders, electronic toys, mobile phones and remote control toys, and add these to the display.

- Create specific places for items within the computer area. For example, put the roamers in their own area so that the children can easily find them and put them back.

- Place CD-Roms together in boxes, or stack them neatly, so that the children can choose their own CD-Roms and also keep them tidy. They can be sorted into themes, such as Literacy or Mathematics.

- Put printer paper into a tray so that the children can feed paper in themselves. Sort the paper into different colours and sizes.

- Ask the children where they have seen computers. Discuss what we use a computer for. Ask the children to draw pictures showing these uses and display them in the computer area with labels.

- Add computer-generated labels identifying the different parts of the computer, such as the monitor, mouse and keyboard. Make the labels big and bold to enable the children to recognise these words quickly and to begin to use the terminology.

- Place plenty of questions on cards in the computer area. For example: 'Do you have a computer at home?' 'Can you turn a computer on?' 'Can you write your name?' Make the questions as visual as possible so that the children can decode the words. Read the questions out to the children.

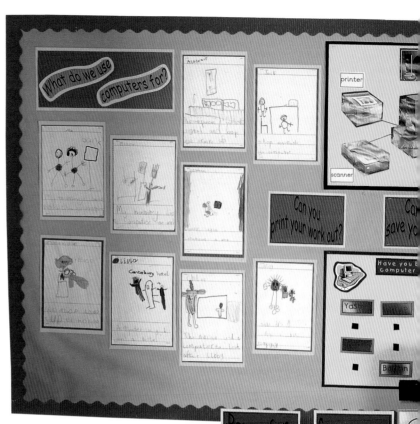

- Highlight a specific piece of software that the children will be using. Display cards which show the children how to use the software, for example 'How to print your work' or 'How to save your work'. Ask the children to design their own cards to help other children use the software.

Safety Points

- Make sure the computer area is a safe place to be. Tidy and sort all loose cables so that children cannot trip over them.

- Always check the equipment within the computer area for safety. Check for loose connections into the computer. Do this activity with the children to show which cables go into the computer. With your help, ask them to fit the cables into the back of the computer.

- Supply the computer area with some comfortable chairs that are the correct size for the table. Try to encourage the children to sit up when using the computer and not to stare at the screen for too long. They should not look at a screen for more than fifteen minutes at a time. A filter for the computer screen is a very good idea as this reduces most of the glare and allows children to use the computer for longer periods.

Using a Computer Suite

- The thought of taking a class of younger children into a computer suite can be a frightening experience for both the teacher and the children, but careful preparation can make the experience rewarding.

- Make sure you have at least one assistant to help the children with any problems. The more adult involvement, the better.

- Let the children visit the computer room before doing any activities. Point out where everything is and let them sit by a computer. Show them how to log-on and log-off. The children should have a username and password to log on to the network.

  ⚠ **Note:** Go through the rules of the room so that they are aware of the safety issues. Ask them why they shouldn't run in the computer room.

- Have a good look at the software on the computers and evaluate their relevance to young children – but, remember to be imaginative!

- Let the children select a program to use or load it for them beforehand. It is useful to begin with a piece of software such as a graphics program that they are familiar with or a CD-Rom that they have used before. This will give them confidence in making the transition from their computer in class to the computer suite.

- Try to design activities that encourage the children to collaborate in groups. For example, ask a group of children to colour in a template in a graphics program, using the 'paint' and 'fill' buttons.

- Above all, let the children have fun on the computers but manage the time effectively so that you can help individual children with problems.

Creating a Role-play Area

Starting Points

- Discuss the importance and use of technology in everyday life. What sorts of technology do the children use at home? Do they use the telephone? Can they change the channel on the television? How do they do this? How do they listen to music at home? Can they change the compact disc in a CD player?

- Make sure the children can record using a tape recorder. Use a recorder with large buttons and glue labels such as 'play', 'record' and 'fast forward' onto or near the relevant buttons.

Office Role-play Area

Include the following items:

- telephone and/or mobile telephone (real or toy)
- fax machine (if you cannot get hold of one of these, ask the children to make one from cereal packets, etc.)
- computer
- answering machine
- trays containing different-sized and coloured paper, envelopes, labels and stamps
- pots of pens and pencils
- telephone directories.

- Display questions in the role-play area to make the children think about the technology they are using. For example: 'Can you write a letter to your friend on the typewriter?' 'Can you use the fax machine?' 'What does the answering machine do?'

Home Role-play Area

Include the following items:

- television
- video recorder
- portable tape recorder or dictating machine
- radio (clock radio or radio tape recorder)
- CD player
- telephone and answering machine
- paper for letter-writing, pens, envelopes and stamps.

A real television and video recorder could be included for the children to watch in the role-play area.

● Discuss with the children the equipment needed in the role-play area. Ask them what pieces of technology they have at home.

● While the children are role-playing in the area, ask how they use the technology: 'What do you press to phone someone?' 'What noise does the phone make when you receive a call?' 'Can you make the radio work?' 'What happens when you move the tuning dial?'

Additional Themes

● Various role-play areas can be created incorporating different technology. For example:

- a library with a computer in it to record which books have been taken out and brought back

- a surgery with computers, electronic heart and blood-pressure kits, X-rays and general equipment used by a doctor. Alternatively, set up a vet's surgery or a hospital area.

Introducing the Computer

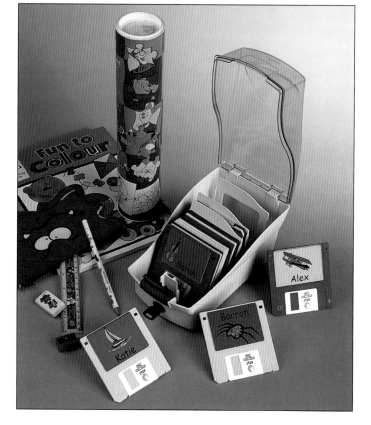

Learning Intentions

- To become familiar with hardware and software.

- To gain basic skills, allowing children to use the computer independently.

- To become familiar with the keyboard and be able to use a mouse successfully.

- To become familiar with concept keyboards and roamers.

Starting Points

- Take a group of children into the new computer area and introduce them to the pieces of hardware. Show them the different items, such as the printer. Open the printer up so that the children can see the ink cartridges and mechanisms inside, but don't allow them to touch anything.

- Show the children the computer. Discuss how they turn the computer on, which buttons they should press and what happens when you press certain buttons.

- Look at the back of the computer and all the leads. Trace the leads to the pieces of hardware and identify each one. For example: 'This lead goes to the printer.' 'The speakers plug in here.'

- Look at the keyboard with the children. Can they identify some of the letters? Can they find the letter that starts their name? Place large, colourful lower-case stickers on the keys to make them easier to recognise.

● Look at some of the basic software packages that the children will use. Show them how to start the program from the desktop, put paper in the printer and print out their results using a specific button. Also show the children how to exit from the program. This will give them the necessary skills to use the computer by themselves.

● Show the children how to save their work and record their achievements by printing and filing. Produce individual folders for the children's work. Print out a title for the front cover, for example 'Rajid's Computer Book' and add a computer-generated illustration or a photograph of the child.

● Split the children into 'colour' groups and encourage each group to work on a set of floppy disks. Place these into floppy-disk holders of matching colours.

● To make disks easier to identify, ask the children to draw a favourite picture or write their name onto their floppy-disk labels.

Developing Mouse Skills

This should be one of the first skills the children develop as it is needed to work most programs. There is a wide variety of mice to choose from, although trackball mice are good for small hands as they have a ball on top which the children can use to manipulate the cursor around the screen.

Use software for developing young children's mouse skills. Any piece of software that requires the children to use the mouse to catch things on the screen and to click on pictures will help them to gain confidence in using a mouse.

Use a graphics manipulation software that allows a character, such as a teddy, to be dressed. Ask the children to pick the items of clothes up and move them around the screen. Talk to the children about what they are doing and allow them plenty of time to practise.

Ask the children to place each item where they think it should go and to drop it by clicking the mouse button. Ask them how they did this. Did they put it in the right place?

Encourage the children to use their whole hand to move the mouse and their finger to click the button without lifting their hand. Many children will place the mouse where they want it, take their hand away and then click the button – a technique which can lead to inaccuracies and a loss of confidence.

Play computer games that require using the mouse as a bat, such as tennis or table tennis.

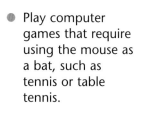

Concept Keyboards

- Use a concept keyboard. These are pieces of computer hardware that allow young children to input words and pictures onto the screen. Keyboard overlays can be made using a piece of software that tells the computer which word needs to appear on the screen when a certain part of the keyboard is pressed. The overlays can incorporate children's drawings which will come up with the word when pressed.

- Use a manufactured keyboard overlay. Let the children press the buttons and see the results. This will help them become familiar with concept keyboards. Allow lots of practice with such overlays before they make their own.

Turtles and Roamers

- Turtles and roamers seem odd to children at first. Before undertaking major activities it is important to give the children time to play with them. Ask questions such as: 'What happens when you press this button?' 'How do you make it go backwards?'

Home Links

Ask parents or carers to:

- use computers with their children at home and encourage their children to bring any examples of their work into school to show the class

- take their children to a library where computers are available and look at CD-Roms together

- take their children to a cybercafé, where they can use the internet.

13

Concept Keyboards in Literacy

Learning Intentions

- To gain alphabetic and phonic knowledge through sounding and naming each letter of the alphabet (using lower- and upper-case letters).

- To link sound and spelling patterns by using knowledge of rhyme to identify families of rhyming words.

- To expect written text to make sense and to check for sense if it does not.

- To recognise printed and handwritten words in a variety of settings.

Starting Points

- Use manufactured overlays that come with some early-learning software. Experiment with the large keys and the directional keys.

- Ask the children to draw an item that has the same initial letter as in their name, for example a gorilla for 'Graham'. Put the picture of the gorilla onto an overlay and use a software program that will put the word 'Gorilla' onto the screen when the picture is pressed.

Activities

- Ask the children to draw a picture for each letter of the alphabet. Incorporate these onto an overlay. Then use a software program to put the correct letter onto the screen when the picture is pressed.

- Ask the children to choose a picture that begins with a particular letter. The children then press the picture that begins with that letter. The letter will come up on the screen to reinforce the child's choice.

- Create an overlay that incorporates words at the top and an alphabetic keyboard at the bottom. Ask the children to spell the words using the letters below. They can press the word first or afterwards to discover the correct spelling.

- Create an overlay with starting words on the right-hand side, for example 'the', 'big', 'boy', 'girl', and the same words on the left-hand side, but mixed up. Ask the children to match the words by pressing them on both sides.

- Use a multimedia word processor to design your own screens.

- Scan some pictures from a book and place them in the wrong order onto the screen. The children must use the mouse to move the pictures into the correct order.

- Insert some words onto the screen and then place the letters that make up the words at the top in the wrong order. The children must drag the letters to the words.

- Create an overlay of onsets and rimes, for example 'cat', 'bat', 'sat'. Include the onset 'c', 'b', 's' and then the rime, for example 'at'. Link the overlay to the computer, so that when children press the concept keyboard, the letters will appear on the screen. Go on to incorporate two rimes, such as 'at' and 'an'. Record the words they have created by saving them into their own files.

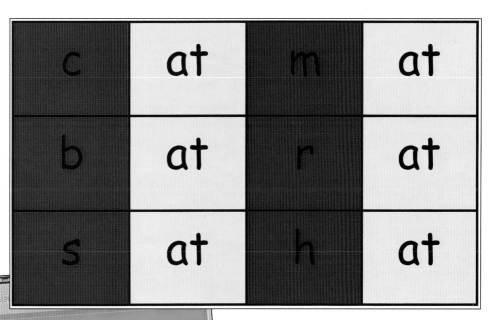

- Set up a multimedia word processor so that when the child presses the onset and rime, the program will say it, for example 'c', then 'at', and then 'cat'.

- Place pictures and words that match each other on the screen. Encourage the children to drag the matching picture to the word.

- Create a screen with the letters of the alphabet on the top half and also on the bottom half, but with all of them out of order. Ask the children to drag a letter from the top half to the corresponding letter in the bottom half. If you use two colours, the dragged letter can be moved to sit on top of the corresponding letter.

- Next, using the same screen, replace the bottom half with upper-case letters and ask the children to match the upper-case letters with the lower-case letters.

- Type in some high frequency words (such as 'dog', 'go', 'went' and 'you') on the screen. Ask the children to match them by dragging a word to its matching pair.

- Place letters on the screen that can be made into consonant-vowel-consonant (cvc) words and ask the children to make up as many different words as possible.

- Place families of rhyming cvc words and ask the children to match them up, saying the words aloud as they drag them together. Two examples of rhyming families are: 'cat', 'fat', 'mat' and 'hop', 'top, 'mop'.

- To extend the use of a simple multimedia word processor, let the children use a normal keyboard to input text onto the screen. Start by asking them to use the keyboard to type their name.

- It is important to let the children have freedom to experiment with a multimedia word processor. Ask them to spell the words phonetically first, and then get the computer to say the word to see if it is the same. In this way, the children can write many things without having to use a concept keyboard. Themes for their writing could include: 'My favourite food', 'My favourite toys'.

- Don't use the spell checker straight away. Let the children use emergent writing at first to give them confidence in using the word processor. Once they have finished their piece of work get the computer to say the whole sentence. This can then be used to check the writing at a phonetic level.

- Once the children have finished their writing, let them play with the size of the writing, the colour and where it is positioned on the screen.

- Ask the children to choose some clipart or to scan pictures from a favourite book. Place the pictures on the page and encourage the children to label them using a keyboard.

- Ask the children to print their work out and put it in their folder as a record of achievement.

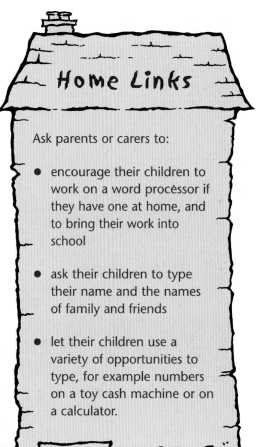

Home Links

Ask parents or carers to:

- encourage their children to work on a word processor if they have one at home, and to bring their work into school

- ask their children to type their name and the names of family and friends

- let their children use a variety of opportunities to type, for example numbers on a toy cash machine or on a calculator.

Talking Books

Learning Intentions

- To recognise printed and handwritten words in a variety of settings.

- To understand and correctly use terms about books and print, for example: book, cover, title, beginning, end, page, line, word, letter.

Starting Points

- It is important to make the transition from 'real' books to talking books as smooth as possible. Allow very young children to become familiar with the organisation of real books first so they know, for example, that the pictures carry meaning and that a book has a beginning and an end.

- Discuss with the children what makes a story. Why do stories have pictures? Why do we have words and pictures together? Which are the children's favourite books?

- Encourage the children to make up some stories on familiar themes. Working in groups, discuss what elements they want in the story, and which bits of the story each child would like to illustrate and write. Each child can complete one page.

- Create a concept keyboard with words and pictures associated with a book the children are writing themselves. The words that the children want can then be printed out and put alongside the pictures they have painted either on a computer graphics program or on paper with paints.

- Demonstrate how the children will use the computer. Show flashcards of the items they will use to navigate the talking book, such as the buttons to press to go back.

- Place the computer in the reading corner so that the talking books are in the same environment as the 'real' books. Remember to use headphones to keep the area quiet.

Activities

- Ask the children to press characters on the screen to see what they say or do.

- Encourage them to click on words that they think they know to check they are correct. Can they guess the meaning of words that they think they don't know before pressing?

- Ask the children to predict what will happen next in the story.

- Help the children to match the words with the pictures. Ask questions such as: 'Where is the owl?' 'Can you find the word for owl?' Try to use high-frequency words in your questions.

- Using the 'real' book, ask the children to say how it is different. Which is better? Which is the easier to read?

All About Me

Learning Intentions

- To promote children's understanding of ICT, other than the use of computers.

- To understand that writing can be used for a range of purposes.

Starting Point

- A good time to introduce young children to cameras is during a visit by a school photographer. Allow the children to observe the photographer at work, pointing out the setting up of an appropriate background, the careful positioning of the subject, the use of a tripod to steady the camera, and how the umbrellas reflect the light.

Activities

- Set up a miniature photographic studio in a corner of the classroom. Create an appropriate backdrop and, if possible, include a tripod, umbrellas, spotlights, clothes for role-play and a variety of old or toy cameras.

- Talk about how to use a real camera effectively: remember to get the head and shoulders of the subject in the viewfinder; try to keep the camera still while taking the photograph; if possible use a tripod to steady the camera.

- Groups of four children can role-play a photographer and photographer's assistant, who take the photographs, and two studio assistants who arrange the setting and backdrop indoors or outside. Provide a large camera that is easy to operate or a disposable camera. Children can take turns to have their photograph taken.

- Encourage the children to write about themselves using a concept keyboard. Make a simple overlay with the appropriate words on it, for example: 'My name is ... . I am ... years old. My best friend is ... .' This can be cut and pasted onto an outline of the person. Use these to make a display entitled 'All about me'.

- Using the developed photographs, cut and paste them onto the outlines in the 'All about me' display.

- Take pictures with a digital camera. Place the picture files onto a computer-generated template. Place labels on top and then print out as a complete picture.

- Take photographs of individual children when they are in dressing up clothes and mount each photograph on a separate piece of card. Make the cards into a book by punching a hole at the top, middle and bottom of each one and tying a string through each hole. Then cut the book in three, horizontally, to make a flip book. Can the class match up correctly the top, middle and bottom of each child in the book?

Home Links

Ask parents or carers to:

- encourage their children to bring in some photographs of themselves or their pets from home (these can be used to begin a discussion on how to take a good picture)

- help their children take some photographs at the homes of their friends and family to incorporate into a school display entitled 'My family and friends'.

Exploring Prepositions

Learning Intentions

- To explore the use of prepositions in a familiar context.

- To explore how to explain the position of an object or person.

Starting Points

- Position the computer so that everyone can see it. Discuss how to access an appropriate program. Use graphic manipulation software that allows an object, such as a teddy, to be moved alongside, inside, behind and on top of other items. The program should also reveal hidden items behind doors, etc.

we found teddy using the mouse

these are some
to describe whe

behind

in front of

HONEY

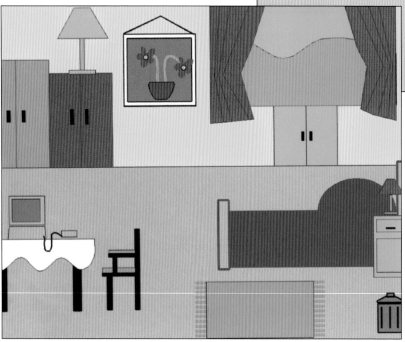

- Open the appropriate screen and ask the children: 'What can you see in this picture?' Encourage them to explain where the objects on the screen are in relation to each other, for example: 'The bed is next to the lamp.' 'The apple tree is outside the window.'

- Ask the children to hide a real object in the classroom for others to find. Once it has been found, that child tells the class where he or she found it.

Activities

- Show the children that they can move the objects around on the screen. Moving an item, such as a cupboard door, might reveal another object. Ask the children what they think it is and where it is. Encourage them to use the words 'behind' and 'in'.

on top of

next to

- Ask the children to try to find a missing object. One child can use the mouse while another directs where they should look next. Encourage the use of correct vocabulary, for example: 'I think it is under the bed.'

- Once the children have found the object, one child can hide it again while the other shuts their eyes. The other child can then open their eyes and try to find the hidden object. Encourage the children to say where they are looking.

Can you find teddy?

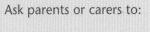

- Ask the children to put the object on the screen back where they found it but to leave a part of it showing. For example, if the object is a teddy, leave a small bit of its ear or foot showing. Print the screens out and ask other children to 'find the teddy'.

- Make a display of the printouts so that the children can search for the teddies again and again.

- Ask the children to place the object in different places around the screen. For example: 'Can you put the teddy *next to* the computer?' Extend this with more complex questions: 'Can you put the teddy *in front* of the bed, and *next to* the lamp?'

Home Links

Ask parents or carers to:

- hide an item and ask their child to draw a picture of where they found it

- help their children to write a sentence to go with the picture.

Messages

Learning Intentions

- To understand the processes in passing information from one source to another.

- To use pictures, symbols, familiar words and letters to communicate.

Starting Points

- Ask the children to take a message to another teacher or another child in the class.

- Discuss the different types of communication there are, such as facial expressions (sad, happy, confused) and body language (waving goodbye, wagging a finger in anger).

- Talk about letters and messages. Ask: 'When do we use these letters and messages?' 'Where do we use them?' 'Have you ever written a letter to an aunt, grandma or friend?'

We faxed messages.

- Construct a robot out of cardboard boxes. Tell the children that this robot can only live when it is fed with messages. These can be written either by hand or on a simple word processor. Alternatively, ask the children to record messages on a tape recorder. Record the robot's replies for them to hear the next day.

Activities

- Discuss what a message is. Ask: 'What should it contain?' 'Should you ask questions in a message?' 'Can you include pictures?'

- Ask the children to write simple messages to each other, using emergent writing or pictures to convey meaning.

- Involve everyone in both writing messages and replying. If possible, include teachers, other staff, helpers and parents.

- Make a set of pigeon holes so the children can post messages to each other. Make sure that all the children get messages.

- Talk about using the telephone to send messages. Use telephones to role-play the giving of a message.

Hi, My name is Letty the robot. Please feed me with lots of words!

Send Your Messages here!

can
Can you

- Use a working telephone and answering machine. Compose answer-machine messages with the children. Then encourage the children to think of an appropriate message and use a tape recorder to rehearse this.

- Discuss what the children need to do to reply to incoming messages on the answer phone.

- Use a concept keyboard overlay to help the children write their messages, for example:
'I can ... skip', 'Can you ... hop?'

- Ask the children to use a fax machine to send their own pictures or writing to other schools. Make a display of the faxed messages that the children have made and received.

- Create emails using an internet connection. Explain to the children that sending an email message is like using the telephone, but instead of talking you can type a message to somebody you know.

- Link up with another school via the internet. Ask the children to send their favourite pictures to children at the other school.

- Create an overlay keyboard so that the children can write simple email messages to their penfriends.

- If possible, use a video-conferencing facility on your computer so that the children can communicate with other children around the world, face to face.

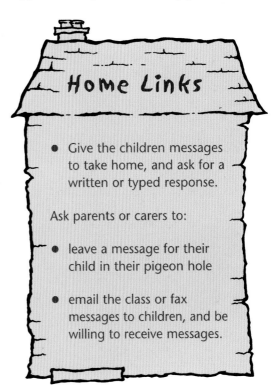

Home Links

- Give the children messages to take home, and ask for a written or typed response.

Ask parents or carers to:

- leave a message for their child in their pigeon hole

- email the class or fax messages to children, and be willing to receive messages.

Roamers and the Wolf

Learning Intentions

- To develop mathematical knowledge and understanding of number, position and size.

- To provide opportunities for practical problem-solving.

Starting Points

- Ask the children to line up in rows. Tell them that they are going to be robots and that they need to do everything that you say. Give the children instructions, such as: 'Forward five steps, turn right. Backwards five steps, and turn left.'

- Ask pairs of children to take it in turns to be the robot and the instructor. Encourage them to give each other commands, such as 'forwards', 'backwards', 'left' and 'right', followed by a number (to indicate the number of paces to take).

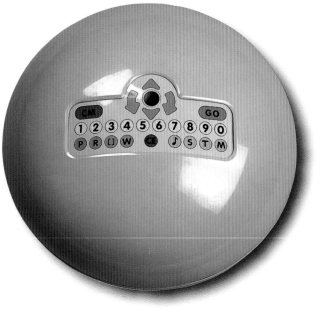

Activities

- Sit the children in a circle and introduce the roamer. Demonstrate what happens when you press 'forward' and a number. Can they guess the number needed for the roamer to travel from one child to another?

- Encourage the children to practise using the roamer with the 'forwards' and 'backwards' commands. Next, introduce the left and right commands.

- Design and make models of Little Red Riding Hood and Grandma's house. Decorate the roamer with painted card to make it look like the wolf.

- Explain to the children that Little Red Riding Hood is lost in the forest and needs to find her way to Grandma's house before the wolf eats her up. Using the roamer as the wolf, ask the children to press the 'forward' button followed by the number they think will allow the wolf to catch up with Little Red Riding Hood.

- Allow the children five attempts before saying that Little Red Riding Hood has successfully reached Grandma's house.

Different Characters

- Decorate the roamer to represent other popular story characters, such as:

  - Postman Pat: The roamer can be made to look like Postman Pat and then be programmed to find his lost cat, Jess, who is stuck up a tree.

  - The Three Little Pigs: Dress the roamer as the wolf again and also make the three little pigs with the children. The children can then program the roamer to catch the pigs or blow the pigs' houses down.

- If you have two roamers, decorate them to look like racing cars and create a start and finish line. The children then have to program the roamer to cross the finish line, using 'forward' and a number, in as many goes as they need. For example, the children might press 'forward' and then the number 3 so that the roamer goes half way down the racetrack. They can then press 'cancel', 'forward' and 3 again so that it will go past the finish line. The roamer that gets past the finish line in the least amount of turns wins the race.

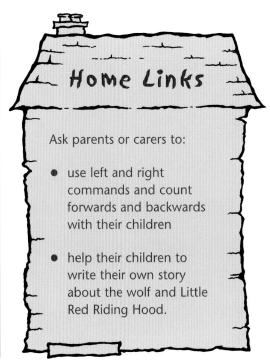

Home Links

Ask parents or carers to:

- use left and right commands and count forwards and backwards with their children

- help their children to write their own story about the wolf and Little Red Riding Hood.

Writing My Name

Learning Intentions

- To refine motor skills using computer hardware.

- To encourage an awareness of own identity and its importance.

Starting Points

- Ask the children to paint their names using different coloured paints and large pieces of paper. Encourage them to talk about the stages they went through. For example:

  - getting the brush
  - choosing the colour to paint with
  - putting the paint onto the brush
  - moving the brush on the paper to make the first letter of their name
  - selecting colours for different letters.

We have been painting our name using a program called 'Paint' We used rainbow colours to write our name

Activities

- Use an art software package that has lots of brush sizes and the option to incorporate stamps (pictures which the children can 'stamp' onto the page). Check that the package has functions to erase and to clear the screen totally, if necessary.

- Ask the children how they write the first letter of their name, demonstrating it by writing in the air with a finger. Help them to trace the shape using the mouse but without pressing any buttons. Let them try this until they are happy to press the button and paint the letter. Repeat for each letter of their name.

We put 'clipart' around our names and then saved our work onto a 'floppy disc'. Can you paint your name using a computer?

- If the children find a mouse too difficult, try a graphics tablet or a touch-pad.

- If the children make a mistake, they can either use the eraser if it is only one letter that has gone astray, or use the button that completely wipes the screen.

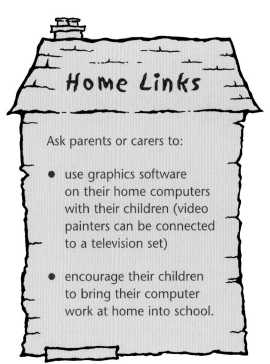

Home Links

Ask parents or carers to:

- use graphics software on their home computers with their children (video painters can be connected to a television set)

- encourage their children to bring their computer work at home into school.

- Set the colour of the paint to 'rainbow' for multi-coloured lettering (see photographs above).

- After painting their name, decorate it with pictures from the art package. Let the children pick the image they want and stamp it onto the paper.

- Print out the decorated names. Open up the printer so the children can see the ink being laid onto the paper.

- Display the print outs along with collage self-portraits of the children. Label with details on how the names were written and decorated.

Concept Keyboards in Mathematics

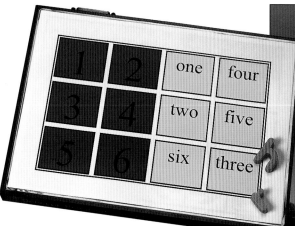

Learning Intentions

- To recognise the numerals 1 to 9.

- To use language such as 'more' or 'less', 'greater' or 'smaller', 'heavier' or 'lighter', and to compare two numbers.

- To begin to relate 'addition' to combining two groups of objects and 'subtraction' to taking away.

Starting Points

- Practise ordering cards numbered 1 to 10 and identifying them. Ask the children to collect specific numbers of objects from around the classroom, such as three colouring pens.

- Using two sets of cards numbered 1 to 10, help the children to match the numbers.

Numbers

- Create a concept keyboard that has the numerals 1 to 6 on one side and the words for the matching numbers on the other (see photograph on page 30). The children should match the number with its word.

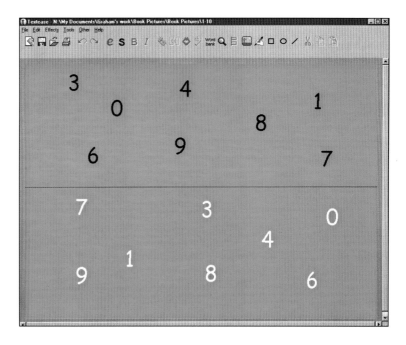

- Create an overlay that incorporates a number line from 1 to 10. Do not print the numbers on top of the number line, instead add empty white squares. Program the keyboard to output the correct number when a child presses inside the white squares. Ask the children to predict the number before they press a square. Can they work out the number by counting up the number line?

- Use a multimedia word processing program to create a screen that contains some of the numbers from 0 to 9 in the top, and repeat in the bottom half. Mix the numbers up in each half (see photograph above). The children must match the numbers by dragging the top number to the matching bottom number.

- Make a screen that contains the numerals and their matching words and ask the children to match the number with the word.

- Incorporate sets of common objects on a concept keyboard. The children must press one set and then press the picture showing one more item or one less item than in the original picture.

- Then, using the same keyboard, count how many items there are altogether in two sets and then click the appropriate set for the total.

- Make a screen that includes sets of familiar items, such as cars, animals and people. Place the numbers '1' to '5' below these and ask the children to predict the numbers in the sets by dragging each number to the correct set. They can then count the items to see if they were correct.

- Create a screen that includes a set of items, for example sweets. Ask the children to drag the sweets to make two sets. Ask: 'How many sweets are in each set?' Drag the sweets into one group again and ask the children to take one or two sweets away from the pile. Then ask: 'How many sweets are left?' Continue with similar addition and subtraction activities.

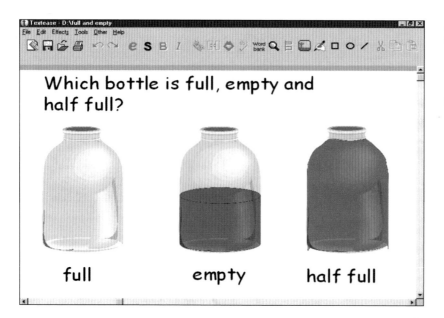

Which bottle is full, empty and half full?

full   empty   half full

- Create a screen which includes pictures of containers that are full, half full and empty. Discuss with the children which they think is which. Add the words to the screen so the children can drag the appropriate label to each picture.

- On screen, use pictures which are either taller or shorter than one another. Sort the objects into the correct order, from tallest to shortest or vice versa.

- On screen, use pictures of small, large and middle-sized items. Sort the objects into the correct order, from smallest to biggest, or vice versa.

- Put three objects of different lengths onto a screen and then ask the children to put the items in order of length. Ask questions such as: 'Which is the longest?' 'Which is the shortest?'

- Place pictures onto the screen depicting typical times of the day, such as eating breakfast and home time. Drag the pictures into the right sequence and then print out.

- Place the days of the week onto a screen and mix them up. Children can put them into the correct order.

who is the tallest?

who is the shortest?

shortest   middle sized   tallest

Which is the smallest truck?   Which is the biggest truck?

Which is the middle sized truck?

- Make a screen that includes pictures of people at different stages of their lives, such as a baby, infant, teenager and adult. Ask the children to sort these into the correct order. Ask questions such as 'Who do you think is the oldest?' 'Who is the youngest?', etc.

- Create a screen or concept keyboard that incorporates basic shapes and the matching words. Ask the children to either press the shape and the corresponding word or drag the word to the shape.

- Make a screen that includes a collection of basic shapes for the children to manipulate to make a pattern or picture.

- Create a screen that starts a repeating pattern and ask the children to continue the pattern by dragging shapes up from below.

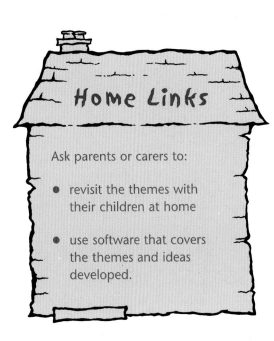

Home Links

Ask parents or carers to:

- revisit the themes with their children at home

- use software that covers the themes and ideas developed.

- Put solid shapes, such as cubes, cones and spheres, at the top of a screen and the names of these shapes at the bottom. Ask the children to drag the word to the correct shape. Use a talking word processing program to get the picture to say its shape when the child presses it.

- Put one shape in different sizes on a screen. The children can then order them in relation to their size.

- Place pictures of different denominations of money onto a screen. Suitable pictures can be found in many clipart collections or real coins can be scanned in. Encourage the children to experiment with these coins by dragging them around the screen. Coins can then be grouped according to their value.

- Place shop items with their price onto the top half of a screen and denominations of money at the bottom, making sure that each item costs only one coin value. Ask the children to drag the correct coin to the value of the item.

Getting Home

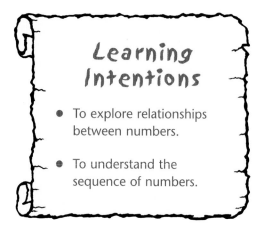

Starting Points

- Decorate a roamer with painted card so that it looks like a spaceship. Design and make a model of the Earth. Tell the children that the spaceship needs to get back to Earth before its fuel runs out or it will drift in space forever!

- Revise the 'forward' command and encourage the children to estimate the number they think should be pressed to get the roamer home.

- To extend the activity, add a few obstacles so that the children have to press the 'left' and 'right' buttons on the roamer. To make this easier, the distance the roamer turns can be altered so that the children only need press '1' for each 90 degree turn. If they want it to do a full turn, they will only have to press 'right' and '4', rather than 'right' and '360'. To program the roamer to do this, press the 'right' button and then the brackets symbol, then type in '90' and the bracket button again.

Activities

- Introduce the children to a *Logo* program. Start the program and type some simple instructions at the command prompt, e.g:

```
TO SPACESHIP
PRINT [FORWARD]
MAKE "N RL
SETPENCOLOUR 0
FD ( FIRST :N ) * 50
WAIT 2000
SETPENCOLOUR 14
BK ( FIRST :N ) * 50
SPACESHIP
END
```

Home Links

Ask parents or carers to:

- encourage their children to estimate distance at home, by asking them, for example, to try to guess the number of footsteps needed to walk from the kitchen to their bedroom.

This program puts the turtle on the screen and asks the children to input a number from 1 to 10. The turtle will move and draw a line corresponding to the number the child entered. It will wait for a while and then go back to its original starting point, ready for the next child to have a go.

- Add a suitable background to the program, such as a starlit sky with Earth in the distance.

- Let the children experiment with the program until they can easily estimate the distance needed for the spaceship (turtle) to get back to Earth.

- Extend the activity by placing the spaceship at different locations on the screen. Start by putting it closer to the Earth and ask the children to get the spaceship exactly onto the Earth. Place the spaceship at an angle to the Earth and encourage the children to think of a way of turning the spaceship to get it back to Earth. The children will have to start using the commands 'right' and 'left'. Let them experiment with the numbers of turn and try to use small angles for the children to turn the spacecraft.

- Ask the children to send the spaceship on a course which avoids the stars. (Place some stars in the way so they cannot achieve this with just a 'forward' command.) Make sure the activity is tackled in groups so that the children can discuss what they need to do and how they are going to do it.

Roamers in Mathematics

Starting Points

● Revise how to use the roamer. Encourage the children to experiment with the roamer to get them used to all the commands. Remember to press 'CE' twice before starting a new program.

● Ask the children questions concerned with distance. For example, ask the children to estimate how many steps it takes to get from one place to another. Ask them to try it. Where they right? How many steps more did they need? How many steps less?

Activities

● Ask the children to build a tower with a given number of bricks and place the roamer or 'demolition robot' in front of the tower. Ask them to estimate what 'forward' value will need to be programmed to knock over the tower.

● Play skittles with the roamer. Label some skittles or towers of bricks with a number and the children have to use the 'forward' command and corresponding number. Extend by experimenting with the 'right' and 'left' commands in order to knock over specific skittles.

● Program the roamer to turn in increments rather than angles, so as not to confuse the children.

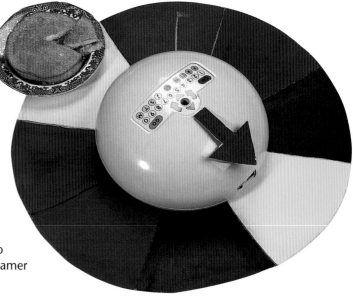

● To introduce turns, make a large pie chart with equal segments of different colours. One child in a pair must pick a coloured segment and the other child must try to make the roamer point to that segment. To make the task easier, set the roamer to turn in 45 degree angles.

- Use cardboard boxes as shops and line them along either side of an imaginary 'High Street'. Make sure the road is wide enough for the roamer to move along. Using the 'forward' command, the children have to estimate the number needed to stop the roamer successfully outside a chosen shop.

- Transform the roamer into 'Romail' and arrange the shops along a 'street', adding the numbers 1 to 10 to each. Romail has to deliver a letter to each shop. Children can pick a card (letter) with a number between 1 and 10 and then program the roamer to deliver it to the correct shop.

- Number lines from 1 to 10 can be made, and the roamer can be used to explore the sequence of numbers for younger children, by using the 'forward' and 'backward' buttons to reach specific numbers.

- Use a number line and roamer to practise basic addition and subtraction. Ask questions such as: 'How can the roamer get to number 10 in two/three moves?' 'What number do I need to say to the roamer to take it back to 0?' 'Pick two numbers – where will the roamer get to if you add these together?'

Home Links

Ask parents or carers to:

- practise counting from 1 to 10 forwards and backwards, with their children

- use remote-control toys like a roamer and ask questions like: 'How many times do you need to press "forward" to take it across the kitchen?'

Counting Cars

Starting Points

● Talk about the different colours of cars the children see on their way to school.

● Which is their favourite colour for a car? Can they predict which is the most popular colour of car? Discuss how they can they find out which is the most popular.

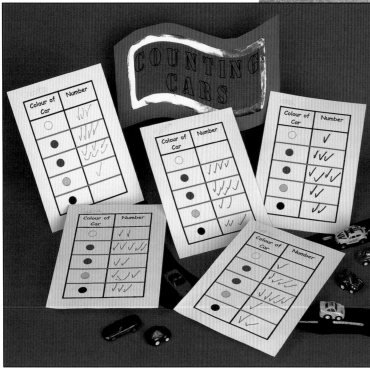

Activities

● Take the children to a road and, in groups, record the colours of the cars going by on simple tally charts.

● Construct a table similar to the tally chart. Each group records the cars they saw. They can do this by adding the number of ticks they have on their own tally chart and transferring the total onto the table.

● Construct a graph using large coloured blocks and photograph it.

- Ask questions such as: 'How many red cars did we see?' 'Which colour car did we see the most of?' 'How many more red cars were there than blue cars?'

- Transfer the results onto a spreadsheet program. Construct a graph with the coloured cars along the bottom axis. Children can transfer their results by clicking on the cars. When they do this a car of that colour is added to the graph.

- Print the results out and display the computer graphs. Alongside, place the photograph of the graph made using bricks. This will show the transition from the concrete experience of data-handling to using the computer.

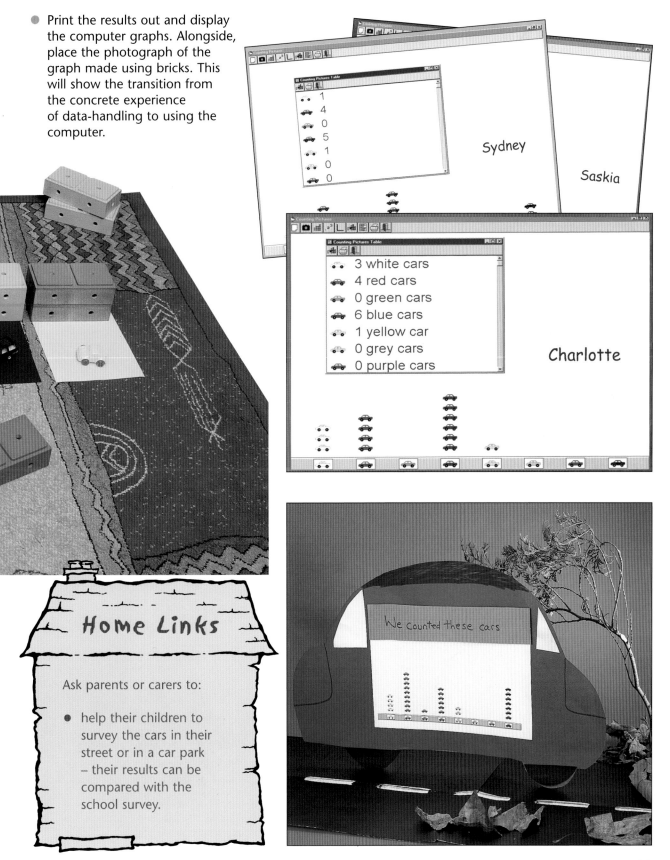

Concept Keyboards in Science and Humanities

Learning Intentions

- To describe simple features of objects, living things and events.

- To observe and describe a range of animals in terms of features such as colour and size.

- To recognise a range of animals.

- To be aware of different types of weather.

Starting Points

- Ask the children to paint or draw pictures of familiar animals.

- Look at pictures of these animals and discuss the similarities and differences between them. Discuss with the children the common characteristics of certain animals, for example, that cows and sheep have four legs but humans only have two.

Animals

- Create a concept keyboard with pictures and the names of animals. Children press the animal and then the word. Program the concept keyboard to output the word when the child presses the picture or the word.

- Mix up the words on the keyboard so that children have to search for the word after they have pressed the picture.

- Investigate what animals eat. Use a concept keyboard with pictures of animals and what they eat. Mix the food pictures and ask the children to press an animal picture and then what it likes to eat (see photograph on page 40). Program the keyboard so that, for example, when the tiger picture is pressed, 'The tiger eats' comes up on screen, and when the meat picture is pressed, 'meat' comes up.

- Look at the different stages in an insect's life, for example a butterfly. Ask the children to draw a picture for each stage. Scan them into a multimedia word processor. Mix up the pictures on a screen and ask the children to sequence them in the correct order.

Weather and Seasons

- Record the weather using a concept keyboard. Include the words 'today is' and pictures of different types of weather. Update and print out a weather report for each day.

- Add a title to the weather report keyboard, for example 'My weather forecast', or an option such as 'I like it when' for the children to record the weather they prefer.

- Use a concept keyboard with winter and summer clothes. Children can match the items they wear in each season. Include the words 'In winter I like to wear', and 'In summer I like to wear'. Program the keyboard to say the words of the clothes when pressed.

- Use a concept keyboard with pictures of different types of homes (house, bungalow, apartment). Include the words 'I live in a'.

- Create a screen that includes pictures of the same scene in each season. Add words for each season. Ask the children to match the season with the word. Program the word processor to say the word when pressed.

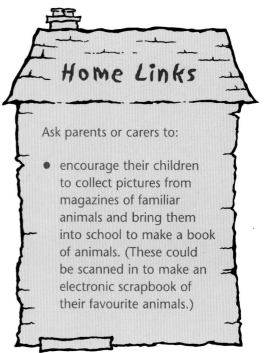

Home Links

Ask parents or carers to:

- encourage their children to collect pictures from magazines of familiar animals and bring them into school to make a book of animals. (These could be scanned in to make an electronic scrapbook of their favourite animals.)

Making 3D Minibeasts

Starting Points

- Take the children out to observe a variety of insects and other minibeasts, such as caterpillars, snails and spiders.

- Ask the children to draw the minibeasts. Use a magnifying glass to observe them closely. If necessary, show the children pictures of the creatures and point out the details. Paint the drawings with colours to match those observed.

worm

dragonfly

spider

grasshopper

- Help the children to print out labels to go with each picture.

- Display the pictures on green card. Cut the card into leaf shapes. Add a card twig and display with model insects and dried leaves, if available.

- Make an insect or spider out of reclaimed materials.

Activities

- Use a graphics program to draw pictures of insects. Make sure the children pay close attention to the features of their minibeast. Allow the children plenty of time to practise – mistakes are easy to erase.

- Print out the picture and glue onto card. These can be hung as a mobile or displayed as part of a poster. Alternatively, tape a safety pin to the back and wear them as badges.

- Make a 3D model minibeast. Print out the children's minibeast pictures twice. Flip the image before completing the second printout so that the picture is reversed. Paint two or three sections of a toilet roll tube or small boxes the same colour as the minibeast printouts. Glue the two printouts on either end of the toilet roll tubes or boxes (see below).

- For a more realistic look, glue tissue onto the toilet roll tubes to fill out the shape of the minibeast.

- Using a multimedia word processor, design other minibeast body parts by importing pictures designed in a graphics program onto the screen. Ask the children to drag together and label the appropriate body parts.

- Search for web sites which show pictures of minibeasts. Print out the pictures and display as a stimulus.

- Ask the children to make books about their favourite minibeasts using a word processor and concept keyboard. This can include general minibeast words such as 'ladybird', 'wings', 'two', 'three'.

Home Links

Ask parents or carers to:

- encourage children who have access to a computer to make up their own three-dimensional insects and bring them into school.

How Do We Grow?

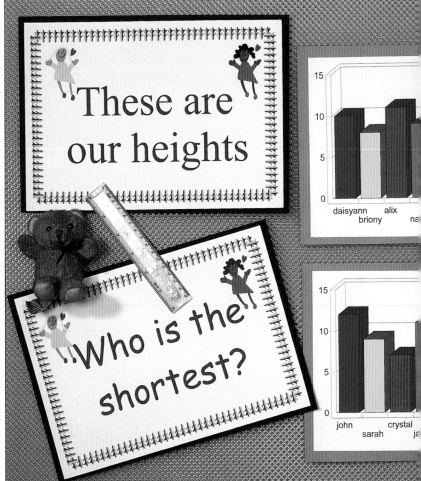

Learning Intentions

- To explore how humans grow.

- To develop the use of simple spreadsheet programs to look for patterns in data.

Starting Points

- Ask the children to bring in photographs of themselves as babies. Discuss with the children how they have grown since then.

- Ask questions such as: 'Do you think you grow quickly or slowly?' 'Can you see yourself growing?' 'Do you keep a chart at home to show how much you have grown?'

These are our heights

Who is the shortest?

Activities

- Give pairs of children a strip of coloured paper that is taller than them. Attach the paper strip vertically to a wall, with the bottom touching the ground. One child in a pair stands against it. The other makes a mark where the top of the child's head meets the paper. Cut the paper strip to the correct length.

- Once all the children's heights have been measured, make a graph to compare the heights of the children.

- Use wooden blocks as non-standard units. Count how many blocks it takes to cover the strips of paper. Transfer the information onto the computer using a simple spreadsheet program that lets the children click on a picture to count up the height of themselves in wooden blocks.

- Once all the children have contributed to the graph, print it out and display it with the other graph.

- Evaluate the way both graphs were created. Which is the easiest to get information from? Who is tallest, shortest? Who is middle-sized?

- Ask the children to line up according to their size. Encourage the children to order themselves to begin with. Ask questions such as: 'Who goes first – the shortest or the tallest?'

- Once all the children's heights have been measured with the paper strips, assemble the strips to make a bar graph. The children can then decorate the paper strips with their own designs.

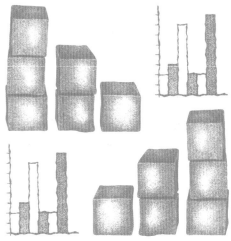

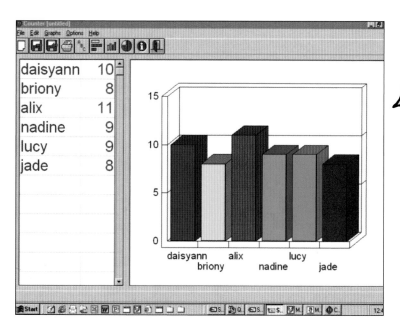

Home Links

Ask parents or carers to:

- encourage their children to keep a record of their growth using a height chart

- help their children to add the information to a spreadsheet.

Using the Internet

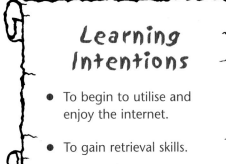

Learning Intentions

- To begin to utilise and enjoy the internet.

- To gain retrieval skills.

Starting Points

- Using non-fiction books, pick a topic for the children to find out about, such as dinosaurs, minibeasts, cars or houses.

- Encourage curiosity about the topic by asking guided questions. For example: 'What did dinosaurs eat?' 'Can you name the minibeasts you can find in the book?' 'Which cars do you like the best?'

- If available, introduce a television text service to the children. Let them explore it before introducing the internet.

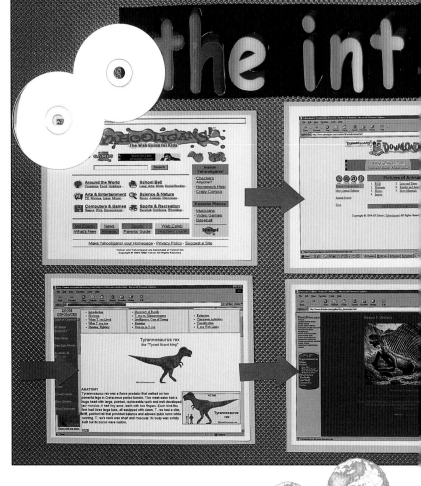

Reproduced with permission of Yahoo! Inc. © 2000 by Yahoo! Inc. YAHOO! and the YAHOO! logo are trademarks of Yahoo! Inc.

Activities

- Children will need guidance throughout activities on the internet as it is easy for them to get lost.

- When successfully connected to the internet, explain to the children that the internet is like a telephone line that lets pictures and writing come down it. This will give the children a way into understanding what the internet is.

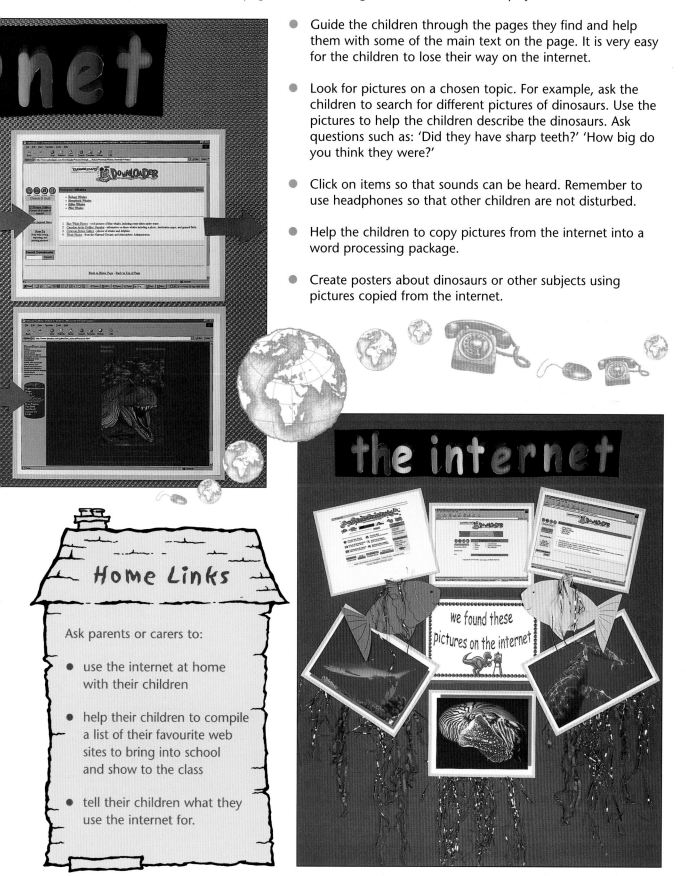

- Using a child-friendly search engine, put a word into the window to search for specific web sites or click a choice of categories. These categories divide into other categories and then specific web pages can be found.

- Print out pages from each stage in their search, and display.

- Guide the children through the pages they find and help them with some of the main text on the page. It is very easy for the children to lose their way on the internet.

- Look for pictures on a chosen topic. For example, ask the children to search for different pictures of dinosaurs. Use the pictures to help the children describe the dinosaurs. Ask questions such as: 'Did they have sharp teeth?' 'How big do you think they were?'

- Click on items so that sounds can be heard. Remember to use headphones so that other children are not disturbed.

- Help the children to copy pictures from the internet into a word processing package.

- Create posters about dinosaurs or other subjects using pictures copied from the internet.

Home Links

Ask parents or carers to:

- use the internet at home with their children

- help their children to compile a list of their favourite web sites to bring into school and show to the class

- tell their children what they use the internet for.

47

Recording Sounds

Learning Intentions

- To explore and use everyday sound recording technology.

Starting Points

- Demonstrate the use of a tape recorder to the children. Use a tape recorder with large buttons and pictorial cues for their functions.

- Let the children record themselves talking. Give them the opportunity to play with the equipment and discover the buttons' functions. Play back the recordings to the rest of the class.

- Ask the children questions such as: 'Does your voice sound the same on tape?' 'Why is it different?' 'Can you identify this voice?' 'Who can it be?' 'What did you do to record your voice?' 'Which buttons did you press?' 'Would you be able to do it again?'

Activities

- Encourage the children to go round the room, or school, and tape anything they wish. Play their tape back for the other children to guess what has been recorded.

● Play games using recordings of sounds from around the classroom or home. The children can then draw pictures to explain the sound. These can be put onto a lotto board and the children can identify the sounds with the pictures.

● Use a tape recorder on a 'senses walk'. If possible, use a small dictating machine which is easy to carry. Before the walk, ask the children to discuss what sounds they might expect to hear. Will they hear an elephant, or a tiger? Encourage them to visualise their walk and the sounds they expect to hear by drawing them on a flip chart.

● Once outside, encourage the children to pursue the sounds they discussed. Ask them where they might find a bird singing, or water splashing. Once they have found a sound they would like to record, give them plenty of time to get a good recording. Leave space between each recording.

● Encourage the use of the rewind button to listen to a recording to check it is good enough. If it is not, rewind to the start of that section and let the children try again.

● Play the tape to a group of children for them to guess what the sounds are. Discuss and explain the steps they went through to get the recordings.

● Paint pictures to explain the sounds they heard on their 'sense walk' and the process they went through to record the sounds.

Home Links

Ask parents or carers to:

● let their children interview them on tape and take their recordings into school for the rest of the class to hear

● tape sounds in the home with their children.

Exploring CD-Roms

Starting Points

- Show the children a CD-Rom and ask them to describe it. What shape is it? What colours can they see when it is gently waved? Discuss what CD-Roms are used for.

- Show the children how to put the CD-Rom into the computer. Ask: 'What happens to the screen when you put it in?' 'Which button do you have to press to start the program?'

- Show the children some of the pages within the CD-Rom. What do they think of them? What do the pictures tell them? Can they guess the title by looking at the pictures?

Activities

- Try a CD-Rom about the human body in which the children can click on any part of the body to gain information through the pictures and animations.

● Let the children explore the CD-Rom. Ask questions such as: 'What does this picture tell you?' 'What do you think this page is about?' 'How do you make the computer talk?' 'What does that button do?' 'How do you turn the page?'

● Ask the children to find out as much as they can about a part of the body, such as their hair. Draw pictures of what they saw and discuss what they discovered.

● Look at a map of your country on a CD-Rom. The children can try to identify where they live. Do they have any friends who live in other places?

● Some atlas CD-Roms allow you to zoom in on a particular area so that the children can see the streets where they live. Ask the children to print these out and place markers on the map showing where their house is.

● Look at a CD-Rom that includes old and new photographs. Ask the children if the photographs are old or new and also ask them why. Is a black-and-white photograph always an old photograph? Why are most old photographs black and white? Did people live in a black-and-white world then?

● Look at the people in old photographs on a CD-Rom. Do they look happy or sad? Talk about how these photographs were taken. How long did the people have to pose while their photograph was taken?

● Design a cover for a CD-Rom that the children have used. Ask the children to include a picture that explains what the CD-Rom is about. Cut the design to the correct size and place over the original cover (see photograph on page 50).

Home Links

Ask parents or carers to:

● let their children take some old photographs of themselves as children into school. How are they different to photographs of children today?

● encourage their children to take a CD-Rom they have at home into school. Each child can share it with the whole class.

When We Grow Up

Learning Intentions

- To use language to imagine different roles and experiences.

- To compare hand-drawn and computer-generated art.

Starting Points

- Discuss with the children what they would like to be when they grow up. What do they think the role would entail?

- What jobs do their parents have? Do they enjoy their jobs? What would the children have to do to get a job like that?

- Ask the children to dress up in the clothes they need to wear for their favourite job. Why have they chosen these clothes?

Activities

- Ask the children to use a pencil to draw a picture of what they would like to do when they grow up.

- Talk about what a person wears for a child's favourite job, and what they would do on an average day.

- Ask the children to write a sentence saying why they want to do a job. How much money do they think they will get for doing this job?

- Look at CD-Roms, such as encyclopedias, that show different types of jobs.

- Use the internet to try to find appropriate pictures of different jobs and any uniforms needed.

- Use a familiar graphics program to draw the same picture onto the computer screen as was hand-drawn in the previous activity. While the children are doing this, ask them which is easier – to draw on paper or to draw on the computer.

- If you have a graphics tablet and pen, let the children use these as they will find them easier than using the mouse.

- Print out the results and discuss the similarities and differences between the computer-generated images and the pencil-drawn pictures.

- Display the results showing both the pencil-drawn pictures and also the computer-generated pictures.

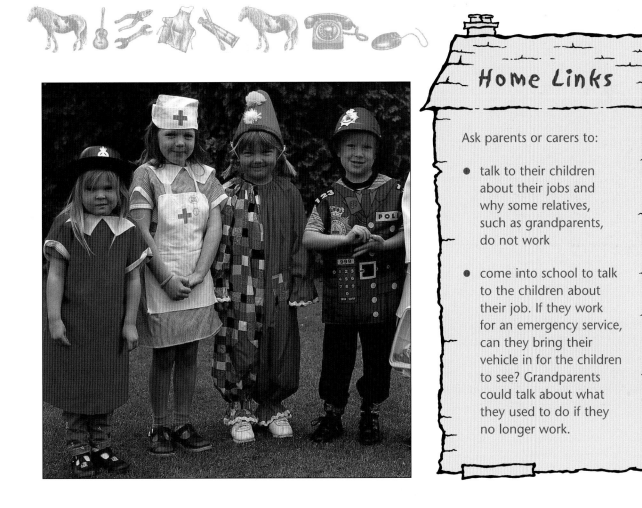

Home Links

Ask parents or carers to:

- talk to their children about their jobs and why some relatives, such as grandparents, do not work

- come into school to talk to the children about their job. If they work for an emergency service, can they bring their vehicle in for the children to see? Grandparents could talk about what they used to do if they no longer work.

Making Music

Learning Intentions

- To explore sounds and different ways of creating them.

- To sustain attentive listening and to respond to what is heard.

- To sort instruments into families.

Starting Points

- Discuss with the children what they understand by the word 'music'.

- Ask them to draw pictures of the things that make sounds or music.

- Ask them who their favourite pop singer or group is and why.

- Ask the children where they listen to music (perhaps on the radio or in the car). Do they have a radio in their house or bedroom? What music do their parents like? What other kinds of music do the children like?

Activities

- Record the children singing their favourite song or nursery rhyme as a group. Later, play this to the whole class and see if they can guess which song it is.

- Let the children choose from a range of musical instruments and to explore the sounds they make. Show them how to record the sounds of each instrument on tape. Listen to the recording. Do the instruments sound the same as when they were playing them?

- Let the children experiment with an electronic keyboard and explore the different sounds which can be made. What is the difference between the white keys and the black ones? (Most keyboards provide help in playing nursery rhymes and simple songs.)

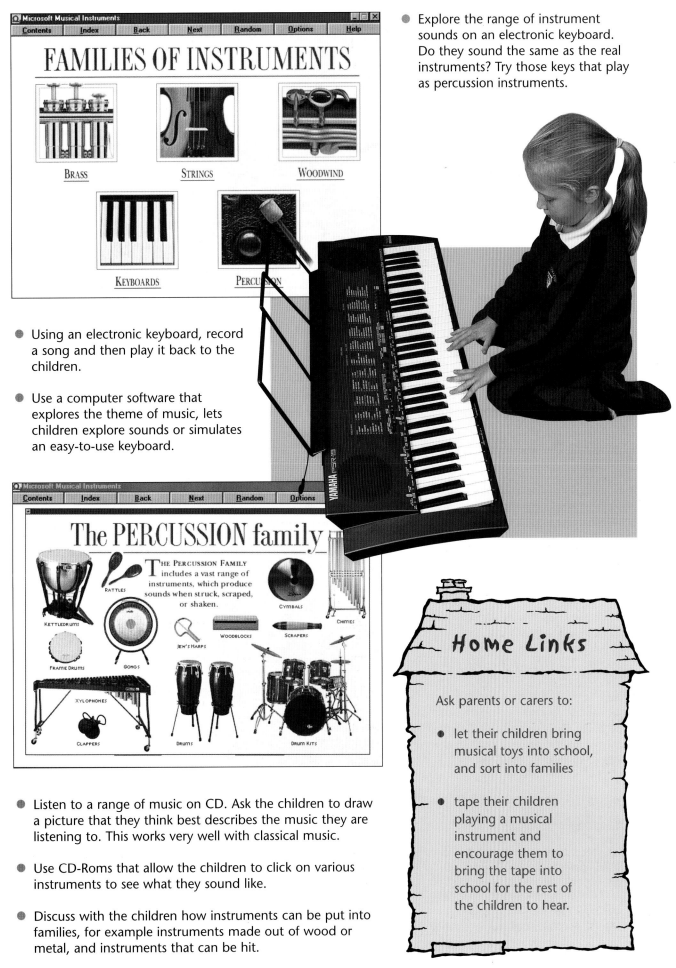

FAMILIES OF INSTRUMENTS

Microsoft Musical Instruments

Contents | Index | Back | Next | Random | Options | Help

BRASS

STRINGS

WOODWIND

KEYBOARDS

PERCUSSION

- Explore the range of instrument sounds on an electronic keyboard. Do they sound the same as the real instruments? Try those keys that play as percussion instruments.

- Using an electronic keyboard, record a song and then play it back to the children.

- Use a computer software that explores the theme of music, lets children explore sounds or simulates an easy-to-use keyboard.

Microsoft Musical Instruments

Contents | Index | Back | Next | Random | Options

The PERCUSSION family

THE PERCUSSION FAMILY includes a vast range of instruments, which produce sounds when struck, scraped, or shaken.

RATTLES

KETTLEDRUMS

FRAME DRUMS

GONGS

JEW'S HARPS

WOODBLOCKS

SCRAPERS

CYMBALS

CHIMES

XYLOPHONES

CLAPPERS

DRUMS

DRUM KITS

- Listen to a range of music on CD. Ask the children to draw a picture that they think best describes the music they are listening to. This works very well with classical music.

- Use CD-Roms that allow the children to click on various instruments to see what they sound like.

- Discuss with the children how instruments can be put into families, for example instruments made out of wood or metal, and instruments that can be hit.

Home Links

Ask parents or carers to:

- let their children bring musical toys into school, and sort into families

- tape their children playing a musical instrument and encourage them to bring the tape into school for the rest of the children to hear.

Rainbows of Colour

Learning Intentions

- To use a variety of media, including real and virtual brushes, to paint and experiment with different colours.

Starting Points

- On large pieces of paper, experiment with paint and various widths of brushes. What sorts of patterns and shapes can they make with the different brushes?

- Which brush do they enjoy using the most? Which would be better for painting large pictures and which would be better for painting small pictures?

- Give the children the three primary colours (red, blue and yellow) and experiment with mixing them on the paper. What new colours can they make? Do they like their new colour? Can they name the colour it looks most like?

- Ask the children to draw a picture of a friend or member of their family. Which brushes do they think will be best to paint the hair, eyes and clothes? Which colours do they need? If they haven't got the colour they need, which colours will they have to mix?

Activities

- Using a graphics program on a computer, ask the children to experiment again with different brush widths. Show them how to select the brush sizes and colours. (Most graphics software allows you to limit the colours on the screen so as not to confuse the children.)

- Explore the different brush shapes and what effects can be created using these. Print out and display.

- Many graphics programs have the ability to cut the screen into four symmetrical segments. This gives children the opportunity to really have some fun with colours.

- Set the colour of the paint to rainbow, so that as children paint on the screen the colours cycle through, producing a rainbow effect. Encourage them to fill the screen using large sweeping movements of the mouse. Do they like the effect? Have they seen this colourful pattern before, for example in a kaleidoscope?

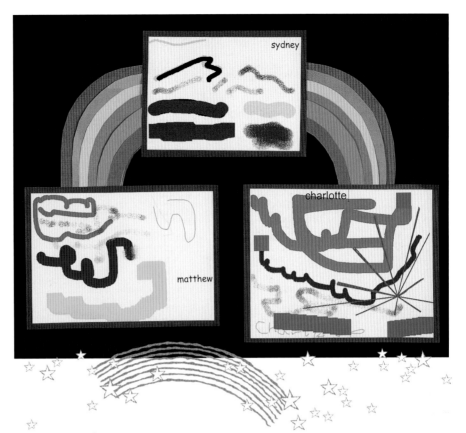

- Ask the children to print out their picture when they are happy with it.

- Display these and discuss with the children how and why the pictures are different from each other.

- Ask the children to try to reproduce their pictures using real brushes and paint. How successful are they? Was it easy or impossible? Display the results alongside the computer-based pictures.

Home Links

Ask parents or carers to:

- help their children to paint with objects other than brushes at home, such as cotton reels, sponges, cloths and toothbrushes.

Butterflies

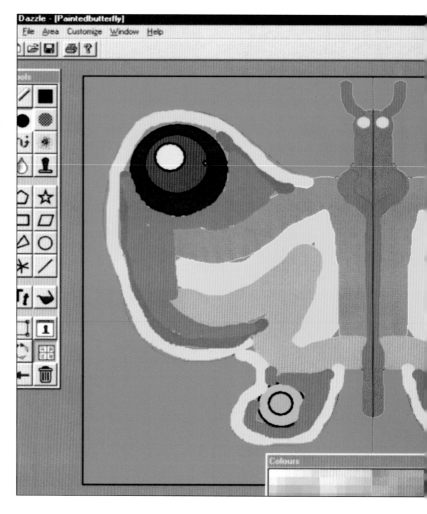

Learning Intentions

- To talk about, recognise and recreate simple repeating or symmetrical patterns in the environment.

- To explore colour.

Starting Points

- Fold a piece of sugar paper in half and draw half a butterfly on one side. Paint the half-butterfly shape with lots of different colours. Before the paint dries, fold the halves together and press down. Discuss the result.

- In summer, go on a butterfly watch. Ask the children to draw the butterflies they have been able to see if, for example, a butterfly settles on a flower.

- Look at some pictures of butterflies. Discuss with the children the different colours on the butterflies.

- Ask the children to draw their own butterflies using their favourite colours. (See photograph on page 59.)

- Look at other examples of symmetry in nature. For example, look at shells, crabs or leaves. Ask the children to paint pictures based on their observations.

58

Activities

- Using a symmetry tool in a graphics program, draw an outline of a butterfly.

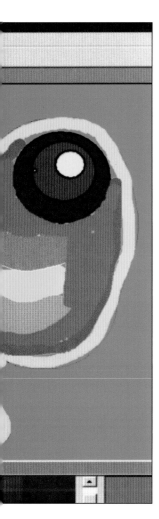

- Drop shapes provided by the program, such as circles, on to one side of the outline. A corresponding shape will also appear on the other side. For variety, ask the children to try different-sized shapes.

- When happy with their butterfly designs, the children can fill in the circles with any colours they wish, but they must make sure that they fill the corresponding shape with the same colour. Complete by filling in the surrounding outline with the colour of their choice.

- Print out the butterfly twice and stick back-to-back on a piece of card for hanging. Hang several from the ceiling as mobiles.

- Attach a piece of string onto the outer edge of the butterfly wings, and then another piece of string onto the bottom side of the abdomen. Hang the butterfly up by the two strings on the wings and let the third string dangle below. When you pull this the butterfly will flap its wings!

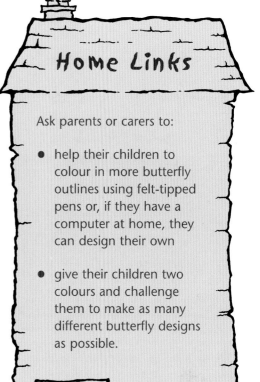

Home Links

Ask parents or carers to:

- help their children to colour in more butterfly outlines using felt-tipped pens or, if they have a computer at home, they can design their own

- give their children two colours and challenge them to make as many different butterfly designs as possible.

- Collect a range of shells, and use a mirror to investigate the symmetry of the shells. Which shells are symmetrical? Which aren't? Make sure that the children are only looking at symmetry in one plane.

- Transfer the design of a symmetrical shell onto a graphics program and ask the children to colour the design using a symmetrical pattern. If possible, use a program that allows you to divide the screen into a vertical plane of symmetry, so that when the children add a colour in one half it will magically appear in the other half, too.

Animal Magic

Learning Intentions

- To experience different approaches to art.

- To use fine motor skills to reproduce a picture on a computer.

Starting Points

- Go on a visit to a farm or zoo, or play a tape or video that shows various animals (wild or domesticated).

- Discuss the different animals the children saw. Ask which were their favourites, which were similar and which were different from each other.

- Ask the children to draw or paint a picture of their favourite animal using a pen and paper. Let them have lots of attempts until they are happy with the result.

We've been making ANIMAL PATTER[NS]

leopard

giraffe

Elmer

a lizard

a sheep

three tigers

Activities

- Look at the markings on animals. Repeat the patterns using paints or by cutting out shapes from coloured card and gluing them onto a coloured backing. Display against a savannah-style background with ferns and coloured paper cut into grass shapes.

● Ask the children to copy the drawing of their favourite animal on screen using a graphics program. Encourage them to explore the properties of the various sizes and shapes of brushes. Also experiment with the spray-cans and other special effects.

● Print the completed animal picture. While it is printing, open the hood of the printer so that the children can see their picture gradually appear.

⚠ **Note:** Don't let the children put their fingers into the printer or get too close in case their hair or clothing gets caught.

● Once the designs have been printed, the children can then incorporate these into various activities.

● Draw a circle around the picture and cut it out. Glue it onto a circular piece of card and cover the picture with sticky-backed plastic. Add clothes-fastening tape so that it can be worn as a very large badge (see photograph below).

● The pictures can be cut out and put onto a large piece of paper. Create text with a word processor and incorporate this onto the paper to make a poster advertising a party with an animal theme.

● Use the printed animal pictures for a display on the children's favourite animals.

● Print out children's animal designs on special iron-on printer paper and then iron this onto a white T-shirt.

● Use an LCD projector and an interactive white board, so that the children can work in a larger area. They can use their fingers to draw onto the white board.

tiger

Home Links

Ask parents or carers to:

● help their children draw animals on a computer at home using drawing software

● encourage their children to explore other media too, such as collage, paint, pencils.

Roamer Patterns

Starting Points

- Ask the children to pretend their hand is the roamer. With a pen in their hand, they should let their hand 'roam' on a large piece of paper.

- Mark arrows for 'forward', 'backward', 'left' and 'right' on flash cards. Working in pairs, one child picks a card and says a number between 1 and 10. The second child has to put their pen down onto the paper and draw in the direction on the card for as long as they think necessary to fit the number.

- Ask the children to bring in remote-control toys from home. Ask them to show the class what it can do and how they do it. In which direction is the toy going? How do they make it turn?

- Paint the tyres of a remote-control car and place it on a large piece of paper on the floor. Let the children move the car around the paper and see what sort of patterns they can get the car to make. Can it make a straight line? A circle? Can it make letters and numbers?

Activities

- Attach a pen to a roamer and program it to construct patterns using 'forward', 'back' and 'around'. Encourage the children to create all kinds of patterns and to try different-coloured pens.

- Once the children have had a chance to explore, ask them: 'What shapes can you program the roamer to make?' 'Can you make it create a square, circle or rectangle?' Encourage them to press a 'left' or 'right' button and then any number so that they discover the higher the number the further it moves.

- Extend the above activity by using a *Logo* program, and then using a concept keyboard attached to it. The children can use this to make their own patterns on the screen. On the left side of the concept keyboard, put the standard commands used for 'forward', 'right', 'left', 'backward'. On the right put 1 to 9. (See photograph on page 62.)

- Brainstorm with the children for ideas on what to draw. An idea, such as a house, can then be taken back to the pen and paper stage or the roamer stage, or it can be tried out on a concept keyboard and *Logo* program.

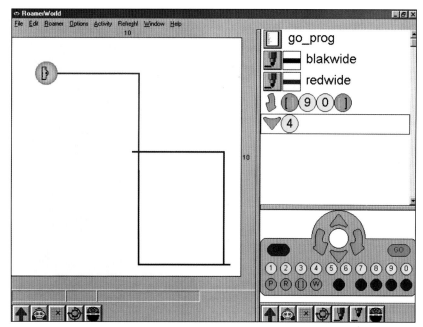

- If using *Logo,* show the commands 'penup' and 'pendown' to the children. This will give the children the ability to move around the screen without leaving a trail, so more complicated pictures can be drawn.

- If available, use *Logo* programs that replicate the command buttons on the roamer. This type of program helps the children progress from the roamer to using a *Logo* program.

- Make some flashcards with some of the more basic commands such as 'forwards', 'backwards' and play a game on the carpet. Ask one child to be the pen and other children to give the 'pen' instructions such as 'forward 5', 'backwards 5' and 'right 1'. This will give the children confidence and help them with the recognition of the words.

- Ask the children to experiment with moving the turtle around the screen. Encourage them to try to solve any problems. Ask questions such as: 'Can you make the turtle go back 1 step?' 'How do you make it turn?' To make the activity easier, program the turtle to turn in increments rather than units of degrees.

- Place some obstacles onto a *Logo* screen and ask the children to navigate the turtle around them. Incorporate a start and finish. Remember to make a 90 degree turn into one unit, so that when the children press 'left 1', the turtle will turn 90 degrees.

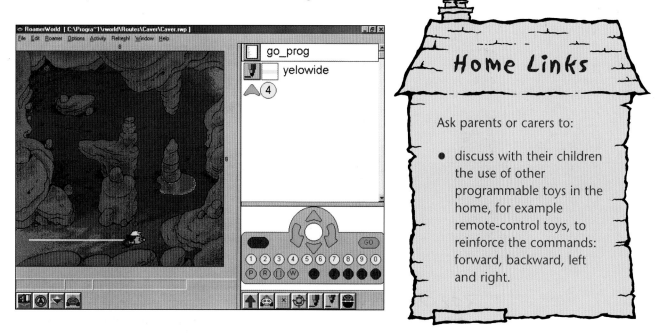

Home Links

Ask parents or carers to:

- discuss with their children the use of other programmable toys in the home, for example remote-control toys, to reinforce the commands: forward, backward, left and right.

Useful Information

Software

● The software used in this book is listed below and is available from leading educational software suppliers:

   – *Textease* by Softease Ltd

   – *My World for Windows* by Semerc Software Ltd

   – *Superlogo* by Longman Logotron Ltd

   – *Dazzle* by Silica Software

CD-Roms

● *My First Amazing World Explorer* – Dorling Kindersley

● *My First Amazing Dictionary* – Dorling Kindersley

● *Amazing Animals* – Dorling Kindersley

● *The Jolly Postman* – Dorling Kindersley

● *Cambridge Talking Books* – Sherston Software

● *Living Books* – Broderbund Software

Web Pages

● www.yahooligans.com

● www.dinodon.com/gallery